A TIME FOR EVERYTHING

mourning and dancing

HE READS TRUTH

EDITORIAL

EDITORS-IN-CHIEF
Raechel Myers & Amanda Bible Williams

MANAGING EDITORS
Rebecca Faires
Jessica Lamb

EDITORS
Kara Gause
Russ Ramsey

CREATIVE

CREATIVE DIRECTOR
Ryan Myers

ART DIRECTOR
Amanda Barnhart

DESIGNER
Brandon Triola

ILLUSTRATION & LETTERING
Cymone Wilder

All photography used by permission.

@hereadstruth

hereadstruth.com

SUBSCRIPTION INQUIRIES
orders@hereadstruth.com

COLOPHON

This book was printed offset in Nashville, Tennessee, on 60# Lynx Opaque Text under the direction of He Reads Truth. The cover is 100# matte with a soft touch aqueous coating.

COPYRIGHT

"We can ignore even pleasure. But pain insists upon being attended to. God whispers to us in our pleasures, speaks in our conscience, but shouts in our pains: it is his megaphone to rouse a deaf world."

–C.S. Lewis

———————————————

God does speak to us in our grief. It is often in our darkest moments that we are most sensitive to His Spirit. Times of grief can be a gift. Instead of letting our sadness wash over us, God's Word teaches us how to look it in the face and actively lament our sorrows. We can cry out to God and implore Him to rescue and sustain us.

God created us as complex creatures, capable of feeling and sensing a myriad of emotions—often many at the same time. As people made in His image, we can grieve the struggles of life even as we savor its sweetness.

It is a mark of spiritual maturity to be able to feel conflicting emotions at the same time—and to feel them both genuinely. Like the immense gratitude and heartbreaking loss we feel at the funeral of a loved one, the juxtaposition of emotions felt in different seasons of life can overwhelm us, but they can also draw us closer into fellowship with our Creator and Savior.

This two-week reading plan will lead us through a series of passages from Scripture that examine the seasons of mourning and dancing in the life of a believer. Our threefold prayer for this study is that you would:

1. Experience growth rooted in the truth of God's Word.
2. Examine your own sorrow and joy in light of Scripture and in the presence of the Holy Spirit.
3. Discover anew the privilege and practice of prayer.

By immersing our hearts and minds in God's Word, and by employing the structure of the laments in the Psalms to write our own daily laments, we will actively practice lamenting our sorrows to God. He is present with us, He is good, and He is faithful.

Read on,

The He Reads Truth team

For additional commentary on each day's reading, download the He Reads Truth™ iOS app from the App Store and choose the **Mourning and Dancing** reading plan, or follow along at HeReadsTruth.com.

HOW TO USE THIS BOOK

Each book in the He Reads Truth Legacy Series™ provides space to read and study Scripture, make notes, and record prayers. As you build your library, you will have a record of your Bible-reading journey to reference and pass down.

SCRIPTURE READING PLAN
Designed for a Monday start, this reading plan is divided into daily readings to help you understand the meaning and context of each day's theme.

RESPONSE
Each daily reading includes space for personal reflections and prayers.

GRACE DAY
Use Saturdays to pray, rest, and reflect on what you've read.

WEEKLY TRUTH
Sundays are set aside for weekly Scripture memorization.

EXTRAS
This book features additional tools to help you gain a deeper understanding of the text.

TABLE OF CONTENTS

"He that lacks time to mourn,
lacks time to mend."

SIR HENRY TAYLOR

HOW TO WRITE A LAMENT

STRUCTURE OF INDIVIDUAL AND COMMUNITY PSALMIC LAMENTS

The three most common categories of Psalms are psalms of lament, thanksgiving, and hymns. Of the laments, there are both individual and community laments.

Psalm 71 is a beautiful example of an individual lament. Notice how the structure of Psalm 71 gives space for complaint (2) and petition (4), but the majority of the lament focuses on God's goodness and faithfulness (1, 3, 5, 6).

The Psalmic lament takes us at our worst, and shows us there is still hope.

1

INVOCATION (Ps 71:1-3)
Addresses God
Expresses a first person cry for help
Remembers God's past intervention

2

COMPLAINT (Ps 71:4)
Describes a specific problem
Conveys an emotional response to the problem
Acknowledges sin

3

AFFIRMATION OF TRUST (Ps 71:5-8)
Confesses a willingness to repent
Expresses confidence in God
Uses phrases like "But as for me" and "Nevertheless"

4

PETITION (Ps 71:9-13)
Appeals for deliverance and intervention
Expresses why God should intervene
Uses words like "save" and "deliver"

5

STATEMENT OF CONFIDENCE (Ps 71:14a)
Expresses certainty that God will hear
Remembers that God seeks restoration and wholeness
Uses words like "hope" and "praise"

6

VOW OF PRAISE (Ps 71:14b-24)
Plans to witness God's intervention
Recognizes that God also laments
Vows to testify of God's goodness and worship Him

INVOCATION (v. 1-3)

Addresses God

Expresses a first person cry for help

Remembers God's past intervention

¹ Lord, I seek refuge in You;
let me never be disgraced.
² In Your justice, rescue and deliver me;
listen closely to me and save me.
³ Be a rock of refuge for me,
where I can always go.
Give the command to save me,
for You are my rock and fortress.

COMPLAINT (v. 4)

Describes a specific problem

Conveys an emotional response to the problem

Acknowledges sin

⁴ Deliver me, my God, from the
power of the wicked,
from the grasp of the unjust and
oppressive.

AFFIRMATION OF TRUST (v. 5-8)

Confesses willingness to repent

Expresses confidence in God

Uses phrases like "But as for me" and
"Nevertheless"

⁵ For You are my hope, Lord God,
my confidence from my youth.
⁶ I have leaned on You from birth;
You took me from my mother's womb.
My praise is always about You.
⁷ I have become an ominous
sign to many,
but You are my strong refuge.
⁸ My mouth is full of praise
and honor to You all day long.

PETITION (v. 9-13)

Appeals for deliverance and intervention

Expresses why God should intervene

Uses words like: "save" and "deliver"

⁹ Don't discard me in my old age;
as my strength fails, do not abandon me.
¹⁰ For my enemies talk about me,
and those who spy on me plot together,
¹¹ saying, "God has abandoned him;
chase him and catch him,
for there is no one to rescue him."
¹² God, do not be far from me;
my God, hurry to help me.
¹³ May my adversaries be disgraced
and destroyed;
may those who seek my harm
be covered with disgrace and humiliation.

STATEMENT OF CONFIDENCE (v. 14a)

Expresses certainty that God will hear

Remembers that God seeks
restoration and wholeness

Uses words like "hope" and "praise"

¹⁴ But I will hope continually

VOW OF PRAISE (14b-24)

Plans to witness God's intervention

Recognizes that God also laments

Vows to testify of God's goodness
and worship Him

and will praise You more and more.

[15] My mouth will tell about Your

righteousness and Your salvation all day long,

though I cannot sum them up.

[16] I come because of the mighty acts

of the Lord God;

I will proclaim Your righteousness,

Yours alone.

[17] God, You have taught me from my youth,

and I still proclaim Your wonderful works.

[18] Even when I am old and gray,

God, do not abandon me.

Then I will proclaim Your power

to another generation,

Your strength to all who are to come.

[19] Your righteousness reaches heaven, God,

You who have done great things;

God, who is like You?

[20] You caused me to experience

many troubles and misfortunes,

but You will revive me again.

You will bring me up again,

even from the depths of the earth.

[21] You will increase my honor

and comfort me once again.

[22] Therefore, I will praise You with a harp

for Your faithfulness, my God;

I will sing to You with a lyre,

Holy One of Israel.

[23] My lips will shout for joy

when I sing praise to You

because You have redeemed me.

[24] Therefore, my tongue will proclaim

Your righteousness all day long,

for those who seek my harm

will be disgraced and confounded.

SAMPLE LAMENT

We've completed a sample lament for you on the facing page. To fill in the blanks, you can draw from the structure we have already explored in Psalm 71. As you progress through this book, use the daily readings to inform and expand your daily lament.

Be creative and use this structure to give you freedom to offer up your griefs to God. This is a sacred space between God and you. Use it to learn to trust Him and pray to Him in new ways.

INVOCATION

LORD, I SEEK peace, comfort, and sleep. I am afraid and worried every day.
(what is your cry for help?)

RESCUE AND DELIVER ME, FOR YOU ARE my rock and my fortress: my safe place.
(what do you know about the character of God?)

FOR YOU give hope to the hopeless, and You are a rock of refuge.
(what goodness has God done in the past?)

COMPLAINT

DELIVER ME FROM my expectations of how my life should have turned out.
(what is the external problem?)

FORGIVE ME FOR depending on my own strength.
(confess your sin; explain the internal problem)

AFFIRMATION OF TRUST

NEVERTHELESS, You are my strength.
(how can you trust in God?)

YOU ARE MY strong tower of refuge.
(what has God promised to be?)

PETITION

SAVE ME FROM fear and a lack of trust.
(from what?)

DELIVER ME FROM my own pride and selfishness.
(what else?)

FOR YOU delight in saving Your people.
(why should God intervene?)

STATEMENT OF CONFIDENCE

BUT I WILL hope continually with the expectation of rescue.
(how can you hope, knowing that God will hear you?)

VOW TO PRAISE

I WILL PROCLAIM how You give me freedom and safety from my fears.
(what will you proclaim about God?)

I WILL SING PRAISE because You have not abandoned me and You have promised to comfort me.
(why will you praise God?)

DECLARATION OF LAMENTATION

....

Grief is a hard and natural part of life. But actively mourning and lamenting to God is biblical and can help us take steps toward healing. Choose a specific thing to mourn, and we will work through the mourning process by lamenting that grief. You can choose one grief for the entire study, or a different one for each day—whatever your heart needs right now. We will examine the ongoing tension of grief and joy through a series of ten themes. And we will prayerfully work through our specific grief day by day as we learn to experience God's healing through mourning and lament.

In this study, I want to lament:

1 A TIME TO MOURN AND A TIME TO DANCE

MOURNING:

Matthew 5:4

Ecclesiastes 3:1-15

John 16:33

DANCING:

John 16:20

Psalm 30

1 Peter 1:6-9

Scripture calls us to rejoice with those who rejoice and weep with those who weep (Romans 12:15). This means we should deal honestly with both the joy and grief in life. We are called to mourn over those things worthy of lament, and we are also called to celebrate the generosity, love, and grace of God.

MATTHEW 5:4

Those who mourn are blessed,
for they will be comforted.

ECCLESIASTES 3:1-15

The Mystery of Time

¹ There is an occasion for everything,
and a time for every activity under heaven:
² a time to give birth and a time to die;
a time to plant and a time to uproot;
³ a time to kill and a time to heal;
a time to tear down and a time to build;
⁴ a time to weep and a time to laugh;
a time to mourn and a time to dance;
⁵ a time to throw stones and a time to gather stones;
a time to embrace and a time to avoid embracing;
⁶ a time to search and a time to count as lost;
a time to keep and a time to throw away;
⁷ a time to tear and a time to sew;
a time to be silent and a time to speak;
⁸ a time to love and a time to hate;
a time for war and a time for peace.

⁹ What does the worker gain from his struggles? ¹⁰ I have seen the task that God has given people to keep them occupied. ¹¹ He has made everything appropriate in its time. He has also put eternity in their hearts, but man cannot discover the work God has done from beginning to end. ¹² I know that there is nothing better for them than to rejoice and enjoy the good life. ¹³ It is also the gift of God whenever anyone eats, drinks, and enjoys all his efforts.

[14] I know that all God does will last forever; there is no adding to it or taking from it. God works so that people will be in awe of Him. [15] Whatever is, has already been, and whatever will be, already is. God repeats what has passed.

JOHN 16:33

"I have told you these things so that in Me you may have peace. You will have suffering in this world. Be courageous! I have conquered the world."

A TIME TO DANCE

JOHN 16:20

"I assure you: You will weep and wail, but the world will rejoice. You will become sorrowful, but your sorrow will turn to joy."

PSALM 30

Joy in the Morning
[1] I will exalt You, LORD,
because You have lifted me up
and have not allowed my enemies
to triumph over me.
[2] LORD my God,
I cried to You for help, and You healed me.
[3] LORD, You brought me up from Sheol;
You spared me from among those
going down to the Pit.
[4] Sing to Yahweh, you His faithful ones,
and praise His holy name.

⁵ For His anger lasts only a moment,

but His favor, a lifetime.

Weeping may spend the night,

but there is joy in the morning.

⁶ When I was secure, I said,

"I will never be shaken."

⁷ Lᴏʀᴅ, when You showed Your favor,

You made me stand like a strong mountain;

when You hid Your face, I was terrified.

⁸ Lᴏʀᴅ, I called to You;

I sought favor from my Lᴏʀᴅ:

⁹ "What gain is there in my death,

if I go down to the Pit?

Will the dust praise You?

Will it proclaim Your truth?

¹⁰ Lᴏʀᴅ, listen and be gracious to me;

Lᴏʀᴅ, be my helper."

¹¹ You turned my lament into dancing;

You removed my sackcloth

and clothed me with gladness,

¹² so that I can sing to You and not be silent.

Lᴏʀᴅ my God, I will praise You forever.

1 PETER 1:6-9

⁶ You rejoice in this, though now for a short time you have had to struggle in various trials ⁷ so that the genuineness of your faith—more valuable than gold, which perishes though refined by fire—may result in praise, glory, and honor at the revelation of Jesus Christ. ⁸ You love Him, though you have not seen Him. And though not seeing Him now, you believe in Him and rejoice with inexpressible and glorious joy, ⁹ because you are receiving the goal of your faith, the salvation of your souls.

WRITE A LAMENT

Use this structure, based on Psalm 71, to write your own lament. Incorporate the truth you read in today's Scripture passages, and use this time to let your heart cry out to God.

*To write a longer lament, use the notes space or use the templates in the back of this book.

INVOCATION

LORD, I SEEK _____

(what is your cry for help?)

RESCUE AND DELIVER ME, FOR YOU ARE _____

(what do you know about the character of God?)

FOR YOU _____

(what goodness has God done in the past?)

COMPLAINT

DELIVER ME FROM _____

(what is the external problem?)

FORGIVE ME FOR _____

(confess your sin; explain the internal problem)

AFFIRMATION OF TRUST

NEVERTHELESS, _____

(how can you trust in God?)

YOU ARE MY _____

(what has God promised to be?)

PETITION

SAVE ME FROM _____

(from what?)

DELIVER ME FROM _____

(what else?)

FOR YOU _____

(why should God intervene?)

STATEMENT OF CONFIDENCE

BUT I WILL _____

(how can you hope, knowing that God will hear you?)

VOW TO PRAISE

I WILL PROCLAIM _____

(what will you proclaim about God?)

I WILL SING PRAISE _____

(why will you praise God?)

2 THE DEATH AND RESURRECTION OF CHRIST

DEATH:
Matthew 27:32-50
Galatians 2:19-20

RESURRECTION:
Luke 24:36-49
Colossians 1:15-20

Before venturing into our own personal joys and sorrows, let's reflect on the foundation of our hope—the finished work of Christ on our behalf. Consider the sadness and brutal reality of the suffering and death of Christ, while also placing that sorrow in the light of the joyous wonder of the empty tomb.

MATTHEW 27:32-50

³²As they were going out, they found a Cyrenian man named Simon. They forced this man to carry His cross. ³³ When they came to a place called Golgotha (which means Skull Place), ³⁴ they gave Him wine mixed with gall to drink. But when He tasted it, He would not drink it. ³⁵ After crucifying Him they divided His clothes by casting lots. ³⁶ Then they sat down and were guarding Him there. ³⁷ Above His head they put up the charge against Him in writing:

THIS IS JESUS
THE KING OF THE JEWS.

³⁸ Then two criminals were crucified with Him, one on the right and one on the left. ³⁹ Those who passed by were yelling insults at Him, shaking their heads ⁴⁰ and saying, "The One who would demolish the sanctuary and rebuild it in three days, save Yourself! If You are the Son of God, come down from the cross!" ⁴¹ In the same way the chief priests, with the scribes and elders, mocked Him and said, ⁴² "He saved others, but He cannot save Himself! He is the King of Israel! Let Him come down now from the cross, and we will believe in Him. ⁴³ He has put His trust in God; let God rescue Him now—if He wants Him! For He said, 'I am God's Son.'" ⁴⁴ In the same way even the criminals who were crucified with Him kept taunting Him.

⁴⁵ From noon until three in the afternoon darkness came over the whole land. ⁴⁶ About three in the afternoon Jesus cried out with a loud voice, *"Elí, Elí, lemá sabachtháni?"* that is, "My God, My God, why have You forsaken Me?"

[47] When some of those standing there heard this, they said, "He's calling for Elijah!"

[48] Immediately one of them ran and got a sponge, filled it with sour wine, fixed it on a reed, and offered Him a drink. [49] But the rest said, "Let's see if Elijah comes to save Him!" [50] Jesus shouted again with a loud voice and gave up His spirit.

GALATIANS 2:19-20

[19] For through the law I have died to the law, so that I might live for God. I have been crucified with Christ [20] and I no longer live, but Christ lives in me. The life I now live in the body, I live by faith in the Son of God, who loved me and gave Himself for me.

THE RESURRECTION OF CHRIST

LUKE 24:36-49

[36] And as they were saying these things, He Himself stood among them. He said to them, "Peace to you!" [37] But they were startled and terrified and thought they were seeing a ghost. [38] "Why are you troubled?" He asked them. "And why do doubts arise in your hearts? [39] Look at My hands and My feet, that it is I Myself! Touch Me and see, because a ghost does not have flesh and bones as you can see I have." [40] Having said this, He showed them His hands and feet. [41] But while they still were amazed and unbelieving because of their joy, He asked them, "Do you have anything here to eat?" [42] So they gave Him a piece of a broiled fish, [43] and He took it and ate in their presence.

[44] Then He told them, "These are My words that I spoke to you while I was still with you—that everything written about Me in

the Law of Moses, the Prophets, and the Psalms must be fulfilled." ⁴⁵ Then He opened their minds to understand the Scriptures. ⁴⁶ He also said to them, "This is what is written: The Messiah would suffer and rise from the dead the third day, ⁴⁷ and repentance for forgiveness of sins would be proclaimed in His name to all the nations, beginning at Jerusalem. ⁴⁸ You are witnesses of these things. ⁴⁹ And look, I am sending you what My Father promised. As for you, stay in the city until you are empowered from on high."

COLOSSIANS 1:15-20

¹⁵ He is the image of the invisible God,
the firstborn over all creation.
¹⁶ For everything was created by Him,
in heaven and on earth,
the visible and the invisible,
whether thrones or dominions
or rulers or authorities—
all things have been created through Him and for Him.
¹⁷ He is before all things,
and by Him all things hold together.
¹⁸ He is also the head of the body, the church;
He is the beginning,
the firstborn from the dead,
so that He might come to have
first place in everything.
¹⁹ For God was pleased to have
all His fullness dwell in Him,
²⁰ and through Him to reconcile
everything to Himself
by making peace
through the blood of His cross—
whether things on earth or things in heaven.

WRITE A LAMENT

Use this structure, based on Psalm 71, to write your own lament. Incorporate the truth you read in today's Scripture passages, and use this time to let your heart cry out to God.

*To write a longer lament, use the notes space or use the templates in the back of this book.

INVOCATION

LORD, I SEEK
(what is your cry for help?)

RESCUE AND DELIVER ME, FOR YOU ARE
(what do you know about the character of God?)

FOR YOU
(what goodness has God done in the past?)

COMPLAINT

DELIVER ME FROM
(what is the external problem?)

FORGIVE ME FOR
(confess your sin; explain the internal problem)

AFFIRMATION OF TRUST

NEVERTHELESS,
(how can you trust in God?)

YOU ARE MY
(what has God promised to be?)

PETITION

SAVE ME FROM
(from what?)

DELIVER ME FROM
(what else?)

FOR YOU
(why should God intervene?)

STATEMENT OF CONFIDENCE

BUT I WILL
(how can you hope, knowing that God will hear you?)

VOW TO PRAISE

I WILL PROCLAIM
(what will you proclaim about God?)

I WILL SING PRAISE
(why will you praise God?)

NOTES

3 SIN AND REDEMPTION

SIN:
Jeremiah 17:9-10
Isaiah 64:6-7
Galatians 5:19-21
Romans 3:23

REDEMPTION:
John 11:25
Ephesians 1:3-10
Hebrews 4:15-16
Romans 8:31-39

Today we will take a more personal look at what the cross and resurrection of Jesus mean for those who have put their faith in Him. These scriptures reveal our desperate need for what Christ endured. Our sin ran so deep, the remedy required the death of the Son of God. Jesus Christ took our sin, paid the wage of death we owed, and then defeated death's very power—so "how will He not also with Him grant us everything" (Romans 8:32)?

JEREMIAH 17:9-10

[9] The heart is more deceitful than anything else,

and incurable—who can understand it?

[10] I, Yahweh, examine the mind,

I test the heart

to give to each according to his way,

according to what his actions deserve.

ISAIAH 64:6-7

[6] All of us have become like something unclean,

and all our righteous acts are like a polluted garment;

all of us wither like a leaf,

and our iniquities carry us away like the wind.

[7] No one calls on Your name,

striving to take hold of You.

For You have hidden Your face from us

and made us melt because of our iniquity.

GALATIANS 5:19-21

[19] Now the works of the flesh are obvious: sexual immorality, moral impurity, promiscuity, [20] idolatry, sorcery, hatreds, strife, jealousy, outbursts of anger, selfish ambitions, dissensions, factions, [21] envy, drunkenness, carousing, and anything similar. I tell you about these things in advance—as I told you before—that those who practice such things will not inherit the kingdom of God.

ROMANS 3:23

For all have sinned and fall short of the glory of God.

REDEMPTION

JOHN 11:25

Jesus said to her, "I am the resurrection and the life. The one who believes in Me, even if he dies, will live."

EPHESIANS 1:3-10

God's Rich Blessings

3 Praise the God and Father of our LORD Jesus Christ, who has blessed us in Christ with every spiritual blessing in the heavens. 4 For He chose us in Him, before the foundation of the world, to be holy and blameless in His sight. In love 5 He predestined us to be adopted through Jesus Christ for Himself, according to His favor and will, 6 to the praise of His glorious grace that He favored us with in the Beloved.

7 We have redemption in Him through His blood, the forgiveness of our trespasses, according to the riches of His grace 8 that He lavished on us with all wisdom and understanding. 9 He made known to us the mystery of His will, according to His good pleasure that He planned in Him 10 for the administration of the days of fulfillment— to bring everything together in the Messiah, both things in heaven and things on earth in Him.

HEBREWS 4:15-16

15 For we do not have a high priest who is unable to sympathize with our weaknesses, but One who has been tested in every way as we are, yet without sin. 16 Therefore let us approach the throne of grace with boldness, so that we may receive mercy and find grace to help us at the proper time.

The Believer's Triumph

³¹ What then are we to say about these things?

If God is for us, who is against us?

³² He did not even spare His own Son

but offered Him up for us all;

how will He not also with Him grant us everything?

³³ Who can bring an accusation against God's elect?

God is the One who justifies.

³⁴ Who is the one who condemns?

Christ Jesus is the One who died,

but even more, has been raised;

He also is at the right hand of God

and intercedes for us.

³⁵ Who can separate us from the love of Christ?

Can affliction or anguish or persecution

or famine or nakedness or danger or sword?

³⁶ As it is written:

Because of You

we are being put to death all day long;

we are counted as sheep to be slaughtered.

³⁷ No, in all these things we are more than victorious

through Him who loved us.

³⁸ For I am persuaded that not even death or life,

angels or rulers,

things present or things to come, hostile powers,

³⁹ height or depth, or any other created thing

will have the power to separate us

from the love of God that is in Christ Jesus our Lord!

WRITE A LAMENT

Use this structure, based on Psalm 71, to write your own lament. Incorporate the truth you read in today's Scripture passages, and use this time to let your heart cry out to God.

*To write a longer lament, use the notes space or use the templates in the back of this book.

INVOCATION

LORD, I SEEK _____
(what is your cry for help?)

RESCUE AND DELIVER ME, FOR YOU ARE _____
(what do you know about the character of God?)

FOR YOU _____
(what goodness has God done in the past?)

COMPLAINT

DELIVER ME FROM _____
(what is the external problem?)

FORGIVE ME FOR _____
(confess your sin; explain the internal problem)

AFFIRMATION OF TRUST

NEVERTHELESS, _____
(how can you trust in God?)

YOU ARE MY _____
(what has God promised to be?)

PETITION

SAVE ME FROM _____
(from what?)

DELIVER ME FROM _____
(what else?)

FOR YOU _____
(why should God intervene?)

STATEMENT OF CONFIDENCE

BUT I WILL _____
(how can you hope, knowing that God will hear you?)

VOW TO PRAISE

I WILL PROCLAIM _____
(what will you proclaim about God?)

I WILL SING PRAISE _____
(why will you praise God?)

4   MORTALITY AND LIFE

MORTALITY:
Psalm 103:15-16
Psalm 90:12-17
1 Corinthians 15:26

LIFE:
Psalm 139
John 15:9-11
Revelation 21:4-5

Today, we will examine Scripture concerning the topic of mortality—the inescapable reality of death, and the amazing gift of being alive. These passages guide us in the art of numbering our days. Consider these wise and sober words as an invitation to anchor our hope in the truth that life was given before death entered the world, and life will prevail long after death itself has died.

MORTALITY

PSALM 103:15-16

[15] As for man, his days are like grass—
he blooms like a flower of the field;
[16] when the wind passes over it, it vanishes,
and its place is no longer known.

PSALM 90:12-17

[12] Teach us to number our days carefully
so that we may develop wisdom in our hearts.
[13] LORD—how long?
Turn and have compassion on Your servants.
[14] Satisfy us in the morning with Your faithful love
so that we may shout with joy and be glad all our days.
[15] Make us rejoice for as many days as You have humbled us,
for as many years as we have seen adversity.
[16] Let Your work be seen by Your servants,
and Your splendor by their children.
[17] Let the favor of the LORD our God be on us;
establish for us the work of our hands—
establish the work of our hands!

1 CORINTHIANS 15:26

The last enemy to be abolished is death.

LIFE

PSALM 139

The All-Knowing, Ever-Present God

[1] LORD, You have searched me and known me.

[2] You know when I sit down and when I stand up;

You understand my thoughts from far away.

[3] You observe my travels and my rest;

You are aware of all my ways.

[4] Before a word is on my tongue,

You know all about it, LORD.

[5] You have encircled me;

You have placed Your hand on me.

[6] This extraordinary knowledge is beyond me.

It is lofty; I am unable to reach it.

[7] Where can I go to escape Your Spirit?

Where can I flee from Your presence?

[8] If I go up to heaven, You are there;

if I make my bed in Sheol, You are there.

[9] If I live at the eastern horizon

or settle at the western limits,

[10] even there Your hand will lead me;

Your right hand will hold on to me.

[11] If I say, "Surely the darkness will hide me,

and the light around me will be night"—

[12] even the darkness is not dark to You.

The night shines like the day;

darkness and light are alike to You.

[13] For it was You who created my inward parts;

You knit me together in my mother's womb.

14 I will praise You
because I have been remarkably and wonderfully made.
Your works are wonderful,
and I know this very well.
15 My bones were not hidden from You
when I was made in secret,
when I was formed in the depths of the earth.
16 Your eyes saw me when I was formless;
all my days were written in Your book and planned
before a single one of them began.
17 God, how difficult Your thoughts are
for me to comprehend;
how vast their sum is!
18 If I counted them,
they would outnumber the grains of sand;
when I wake up, I am still with You.
19 God, if only You would kill the wicked—
you bloodthirsty men, stay away from me—
20 who invoke You deceitfully.
Your enemies swear by You falsely.
21 LORD, don't I hate those who hate You,
and detest those who rebel against You?
22 I hate them with extreme hatred;
I consider them my enemies.
23 Search me, God, and know my heart;
test me and know my concerns.
24 See if there is any offensive way in me;
lead me in the everlasting way.

JOHN 15:9-11

9 "As the Father has loved Me, I have also loved you. Remain in My love. 10 If you keep My commands you will remain in My love, just as I have kept My Father's commands and remain in His love. 11 I have spoken these things to you so that My joy may be in you and your joy may be complete."

REVELATION 21:4-5

4 He will wipe away every tear from their eyes. Death will no longer exist; grief, crying, and pain will exist no longer, because the previous things have passed away. 5 Then the One seated on the throne said, "Look! I am making everything new." He also said, "Write, because these words are faithful and true."

WRITE A LAMENT

Use this structure, based on Psalm 71, to write your own lament. Incorporate the truth you read in today's Scripture passages, and use this time to let your heart cry out to God.

*To write a longer lament, use the notes space or use the templates in the back of this book.

INVOCATION

LORD, I SEEK _____
(what is your cry for help?)

RESCUE AND DELIVER ME, FOR YOU ARE _____
(what do you know about the character of God?)

FOR YOU _____
(what goodness has God done in the past?)

COMPLAINT

DELIVER ME FROM _____
(what is the external problem?)

FORGIVE ME FOR _____
(confess your sin; explain the internal problem)

AFFIRMATION OF TRUST

NEVERTHELESS, _____
(how can you trust in God?)

YOU ARE MY _____
(what has God promised to be?)

PETITION

SAVE ME FROM _____
(from what?)

DELIVER ME FROM _____
(what else?)

FOR YOU _____
(why should God intervene?)

STATEMENT OF CONFIDENCE

BUT I WILL _____
(how can you hope, knowing that God will hear you?)

VOW TO PRAISE

I WILL PROCLAIM _____
(what will you proclaim about God?)

I WILL SING PRAISE _____
(why will you praise God?)

5   GRIEF AND REMEMBRANCE

GRIEF:
Jeremiah 8:18
Psalm 42
Genesis 23:1-4, 19

REMEMBRANCE:
Isaiah 25:8
Psalm 43
Isaiah 65:19-20

Today's readings remind us of the importance of acknowledging the specific losses we experience in our lives, and not trying to rush past our sorrow too quickly. There is a time to weep and grieve, and we should allow ourselves that time. The grieving process includes not only sadness, but also celebration of the life and love of those we've lost.

JEREMIAH 8:18

My joy has flown away;

grief has settled on me.

My heart is sick.

PSALM 42

Longing for God

[1] As a deer longs for streams of water,

so I long for You, God.

[2] I thirst for God, the living God.

When can I come and appear before God?

[3] My tears have been my food day and night,

while all day long people say to me,

"Where is your God?"

[4] I remember this as I pour out my heart:

how I walked with many,

leading the festive procession to the house of God,

with joyful and thankful shouts.

[5] Why am I so depressed?

Why this turmoil within me?

Put your hope in God, for I will still praise Him,

my Savior and my God.

[6] I am deeply depressed;

therefore I remember You from the land of Jordan

and the peaks of Hermon, from Mount Mizar.

[7] Deep calls to deep in the roar of Your waterfalls;

all Your breakers and Your billows have swept over me.

[8] The LORD will send His faithful love by day;

His song will be with me in the night—

a prayer to the God of my life.

⁹ I will say to God, my rock,

"Why have You forgotten me?

Why must I go about in sorrow

because of the enemy's oppression?"

¹⁰ My adversaries taunt me,

as if crushing my bones,

while all day long they say to me,

"Where is your God?"

¹¹ Why am I so depressed?

Why this turmoil within me?

Put your hope in God, for I will still praise

Him,

my Savior and my God.

GENESIS 23:1-4, 19

¹ Now Sarah lived 127 years; these were all the years of her life. ² Sarah died in Kiriath-arba (that is, Hebron) in the land of Canaan, and Abraham went to mourn for Sarah and to weep for her. ³ Then Abraham got up from beside his dead wife and spoke to the Hittites: ⁴ "I am a foreign resident among you. Give me a burial site among you so that I can bury my dead."

…

¹⁹ After this, Abraham buried his wife Sarah in the cave of the field at Machpelah near Mamre (that is, Hebron) in the land of Canaan.

REMEMBRANCE

ISAIAH 25:8

He will destroy death forever.

The LORD God will wipe away the tears

from every face

and remove His people's disgrace

from the whole earth,

for the LORD has spoken.

PSALM 43

¹ Vindicate me, God, and defend my cause

against an ungodly nation;

rescue me from the deceitful and unjust

man.

² For You are the God of my refuge.

Why have You rejected me?

Why must I go about in sorrow

because of the enemy's oppression?

³ Send Your light and Your truth; let them

lead me.

Let them bring me to Your holy mountain,

to Your dwelling place.

⁴ Then I will come to the altar of God,

to God, my greatest joy.

I will praise You with the lyre,

God, my God.

⁵ Why am I so depressed?

Why this turmoil within me?

Put your hope in God, for I will still praise
Him,
my Savior and my God.

ISAIAH 65:19-20

[19] "I will rejoice in Jerusalem
and be glad in My people.
The sound of weeping and crying
will no longer be heard in her.
[20] In her, a nursing infant will no longer live
only a few days,
or an old man not live out his days.
Indeed, the youth will die at a hundred years,
and the one who misses a hundred years will be cursed."

WRITE A LAMENT

Use this structure, based on Psalm 71, to write your own lament. Incorporate the truth you read in today's Scripture passages, and use this time to let your heart cry out to God.

*To write a longer lament, use the notes space or use the templates in the back of this book.

INVOCATION

LORD, I SEEK _____
(what is your cry for help?)

RESCUE AND DELIVER ME, FOR YOU ARE _____
(what do you know about the character of God?)

FOR YOU _____
(what goodness has God done in the past?)

COMPLAINT

DELIVER ME FROM _____
(what is the external problem?)

FORGIVE ME FOR _____
(confess your sin; explain the internal problem)

AFFIRMATION OF TRUST

NEVERTHELESS, _____
(how can you trust in God?)

YOU ARE MY _____
(what has God promised to be?)

PETITION

SAVE ME FROM _____
(from what?)

DELIVER ME FROM _____
(what else?)

FOR YOU _____
(why should God intervene?)

STATEMENT OF CONFIDENCE

BUT I WILL _____
(how can you hope, knowing that God will hear you?)

VOW TO PRAISE

I WILL PROCLAIM _____
(what will you proclaim about God?)

I WILL SING PRAISE _____
(why will you praise God?)

6 GRACE DAY

Use this day to pray, rest, and reflect on this week's reading, giving thanks for the grace that is ours in Christ.

Focusing on the first part of verse 4, ask the Holy Spirit for the freedom to weep and to laugh in every season of your life.

There is an occasion for everything,
and a time for every activity under
heaven:

a time to weep and a time to laugh;
a time to mourn and a time to dance.

ECCLESIASTES 3:1,4

7 | WEEKLY TRUTH

Scripture is God-breathed and true. When we memorize it, we carry the gospel with us wherever we go.

"I assure you: You will weep and wail, but the world will rejoice. You will become sorrowful, but your sorrow will turn to joy."

weep with those who weep

HOW TO HELP A FRIEND THROUGH LOSS

One of the most common causes for mourning is the death of a loved one. Sometimes the loss is personal, but more often, we find ourselves wondering how to live out the Bible's instructions to "weep with those who weep." The following are practical suggestions from Nancy Guthrie's book, *What Grieving People Wish You Knew About What Really Helps (and What Really Hurts)*.

ABOUT NANCY

Nancy Guthrie teaches the Bible at her home church in Franklin, Tennessee, as well as through books, videos, and conferences. In addition to hosting Respite Retreats with her husband, David, for couples who have faced the death of child, Nancy offers biblical insight to the grieving through the *GriefShare* video series and through books such as *Holding on to Hope* and *Hearing Jesus Speak into Your Sorrow*.

SIX WAYS TO SAY "HOW ARE YOU?"
TO A GRIEVING PERSON:

1 | *What is your grief like these days?* This question assumes that it makes sense that the person is sad and gives them the opportunity to talk about it.

2 | *I can't imagine how hard it must be to face these days without (name of person who died). Are there particular times of day you're finding especially hard?* Keep on saying the name of the person who died. It is music to the grieving person's ears.

3 | *I find myself really missing (name of person who died) lately.* It is a great comfort for the grieving person to know that she is not the only one who misses them.

4 | *I often think of you when I'm (gardening/driving by your house/going for a walk/getting up in the morning/etc.) and whisper a prayer for you to experience God's comfort. Are there particular things I could be praying for you?*

5 | *I know that (name of the person who died)'s birthday/deathday is coming up and it must be so very hard to anticipate that day without him/her here. How can I honor their memory with you?*

6 | *I know (a holiday, birthday, anniversary) is coming up and it must be so hard to anticipate that day without him/her here. Is there anything I could do to help you get through that day?*

SHOW UP

Don't disappear. Don't avoid.

LISTEN MORE THAN YOU TALK

Resist interrupting, correcting, fixing, advice-giving, and judging.

WEEP

Your tears don't add to their sorrow; they demonstrate they are not alone.

LAUGH

Be a safe person to laugh with by not assuming that their laughter means they are done with their sorrow.

LEAVE A MESSAGE

A grieving person may not want to answer the phone. Leave caring words for them to listen to again and again.

SEND A NOTE

And then another.

SUPPLY PRACTICAL NEEDS

Bring food in disposable containers, meal delivery from a favorite restaurant, or paper products so they don't have to do dishes. Volunteer to run errands.

MARK YOUR CALENDAR

Make a note on your calendar to reach out on days that might be hard, such as birthdays, deathdays, or holidays.

INVITE BUT DON'T PUSH

Grieving people often feel like they don't fit in anymore. They need gentle encouragement to return to life with friends.

BE PATIENT

Just as time is necessary in the healing of a physical injury, we cannot hurry the process of emotional healing.

EASE THE FINANCIAL BURDEN

Financial strain on top of heartache can be especially difficult. Consider some costs you may be able to help cover.

POINT THEM TO CHRIST

Pray with them and for them, and leave room for them to lean into the Comforter.

OFFER TO HELP WITH THE HARD STUFF

Ask what hard thing they need to do but can't—picking out clothes for burial, cleaning out a closet, writing thank-you notes—and offer to do it with them or for them.

COMMIT TO BEING THERE OVER THE LONG HAUL

Grieving people need friends who aren't going anywhere.

8

WEEPING AND REJOICING WITH OTHERS

WEEPING:

Psalm 22:24

John 11:28-44

1 Thessalonians 4:13-18

Matthew 11:28

REJOICING:

Romans 12:12-15

Hebrews 10:24-25

2 Corinthians 1:3-7

What does it mean to weep with those who weep and rejoice with those who rejoice? Today we shift our focus from our own personal mourning and dancing to the sorrows and celebrations of others. It is important that we learn to do both—lament other people's heartaches and celebrate other people's joys. These Scriptures help us know how to walk with others through their seasons of grief and celebration.

PSALM 22:24

For He has not despised or detested
the torment of the afflicted.
He did not hide His face from him
but listened when he cried to Him for help.

JOHN 11:28-44

Jesus Shares the Sorrows of Death

[28] Having said this, she went back and called her sister Mary, saying in private, "The Teacher is here and is calling for you."

[29] As soon as she heard this, she got up quickly and went to Him. [30] Jesus had not yet come into the village but was still in the place where Martha had met Him. [31] The Jews who were with her in the house consoling her saw that Mary got up quickly and went out. So they followed her, supposing that she was going to the tomb to cry there.

[32] When Mary came to where Jesus was and saw Him, she fell at His feet and told Him, "Lord, if You had been here, my brother would not have died!"

[33] When Jesus saw her crying, and the Jews who had come with her crying, He was angry in His spirit and deeply moved. [34] "Where have you put him?" He asked.

"Lord," they told Him, "come and see."

[35] Jesus wept.

[36] So the Jews said, "See how He loved him!" [37] But some of them said, "Couldn't He who opened the blind man's eyes also have kept this man from dying?"

[38] Then Jesus, angry in Himself again, came to the tomb. It was a cave, and a stone was lying against it. [39] "Remove the stone," Jesus said.

Martha, the dead man's sister, told Him, "Lord, he's already decaying. It's been four days."

[40] Jesus said to her, "Didn't I tell you that if you believed you would see the glory of God?"

[41] So they removed the stone. Then Jesus raised His eyes and said, "Father, I thank You that You heard Me. [42] I know that You always hear Me, but because of the crowd standing here I said this, so they may believe You sent Me." [43] After He said this, He shouted with a loud voice, "Lazarus, come out!" [44] The dead man came out bound hand and foot with linen strips and with his face wrapped in a cloth. Jesus said to them, "Loose him and let him go."

1 THESSALONIANS 4:13-18

[13] We do not want you to be uninformed, brothers, concerning those who are asleep, so that you will not grieve like the rest, who have no hope. [14] Since we believe that Jesus died and rose again, in the same way God will bring with Him those who have fallen asleep through Jesus. [15] For we say this to you by a revelation from the Lord: We who are still alive at the Lord's coming will certainly have no advantage over those who have fallen asleep. [16] For the Lord Himself will descend from heaven with a shout, with the archangel's voice, and with the trumpet of God, and the dead in Christ will rise first. [17] Then we who are still alive will be caught up together

with them in the clouds to meet the LORD in the air and so we will always be with the LORD. [18] Therefore encourage one another with these words.

MATTHEW 11:28

"Come to Me, all of you who are weary and burdened, and I will give you rest."

REJOICING WITH OTHERS

ROMANS 12:12-15

[12] Rejoice in hope; be patient in affliction; be persistent in prayer. [13] Share with the saints in their needs; pursue hospitality. [14] Bless those who persecute you; bless and do not curse. [15] Rejoice with those who rejoice; weep with those who weep.

HEBREWS 10:24-25

[24] And let us be concerned about one another in order to promote love and good works, [25] not staying away from our worship meetings, as some habitually do, but encouraging each other, and all the more as you see the day drawing near.

2 CORINTHIANS 1:3-7

[3] Praise the God and Father of our LORD Jesus Christ, the Father of mercies and the God of all comfort. [4] He comforts us in all our affliction, so that we may be able to comfort those who are in any kind of affliction, through the comfort we ourselves receive from God. [5] For as the sufferings of Christ overflow to us, so through Christ our comfort also overflows. [6] If we are afflicted, it is for your comfort and salvation. If we are comforted, it is for your comfort, which is experienced in your endurance of the same sufferings that we suffer. [7] And our hope for you is firm, because we know that as you share in the sufferings, so you will share in the comfort.

WRITE A LAMENT

Use this structure, based on Psalm 71, to write your own lament. Incorporate the truth you read in today's Scripture passages, and use this time to let your heart cry out to God.

*To write a longer lament, use the notes space or use the templates in the back of this book.

INVOCATION

LORD, I SEEK _____
(what is your cry for help?)

RESCUE AND DELIVER ME, FOR YOU ARE _____
(what do you know about the character of God?)

FOR YOU _____
(what goodness has God done in the past?)

COMPLAINT

DELIVER ME FROM _____
(what is the external problem?)

FORGIVE ME FOR _____
(confess your sin; explain the internal problem)

AFFIRMATION OF TRUST

NEVERTHELESS, _____
(how can you trust in God?)

YOU ARE MY _____
(what has God promised to be?)

PETITION

SAVE ME FROM _____
(from what?)

DELIVER ME FROM _____
(what else?)

FOR YOU _____
(why should God intervene?)

STATEMENT OF CONFIDENCE

BUT I WILL _____
(how can you hope, knowing that God will hear you?)

VOW TO PRAISE

I WILL PROCLAIM _____
(what will you proclaim about God?)

I WILL SING PRAISE _____
(why will you praise God?)

9   AFFLICTION AND HEALING

AFFLICTION:
Mark 2:17
Mark 1:40-42
2 Corinthians 12:5-10
Psalm 34:19

HEALING:
Psalm 147:3
Matthew 14:14
1 Peter 2:24
2 Corinthians 4:7-18

We live in a fractured world with bodies that break down. Yet our bodies are amazing creations which bear the image of God. Today's scriptures lead us through lamenting the reality of our physical limits— which we all have, from seasonal allergies to chronic illness— even as those limits anchor us to the compassion and healing Christ offers to those who suffer. Whether through healing in this life or the eternal healing that belongs to those who are in Christ, there will come a day when all our afflictions will cease.

MARK 2:17

When Jesus heard this, He told them, "Those who are well don't need a doctor, but the sick do need one. I didn't come to call the righteous, but sinners."

MARK 1:40-42

40 Then a man with a serious skin disease came to Him and, on his knees, begged Him: "If You are willing, You can make me clean."

41 Moved with compassion, Jesus reached out His hand and touched him. "I am willing," He told him. "Be made clean." 42 Immediately the disease left him, and he was healed.

2 CORINTHIANS 12:5-10

5 I will boast about this person, but not about myself, except of my weaknesses. 6 For if I want to boast, I will not be a fool, because I will be telling the truth. But I will spare you, so that no one can credit me with something beyond what he sees in me or hears from me, 7 especially because of the extraordinary revelations. Therefore, so that I would not exalt myself, a thorn in the flesh was given to me, a messenger of Satan to torment me so I would not exalt myself. 8 Concerning this, I pleaded with the LORD three times to take it away from me. 9 But He said to me, "My grace is sufficient for you, for power is perfected in weakness." Therefore, I will most gladly boast all the more about my weaknesses, so that Christ's power may reside in me. 10 So I take pleasure in weaknesses, insults, catastrophes, persecutions, and in pressures, because of Christ. For when I am weak, then I am strong.

PSALM 34:19

Many adversities come to the one who is righteous,
but the LORD delivers him from them all.

HEALING

PSALM 147:3

He heals the brokenhearted
and binds up their wounds.

MATTHEW 14:14

As He stepped ashore, He saw a huge crowd, felt compassion for them,
and healed their sick.

1 PETER 2:24

He Himself bore our sins
in His body on the tree,
so that, having died to sins,
we might live for righteousness;
you have been healed by His wounds.

2 CORINTHIANS 4:7-18

Treasure in Clay Jars

[7] Now we have this treasure in clay jars, so that this extraordinary power may be from God and not from us. [8] We are pressured in every way but not crushed; we are perplexed but not in despair; [9] we are persecuted but not abandoned; we are struck down but not destroyed. [10] We always carry the death of Jesus in our body, so that

the life of Jesus may also be revealed in our body. [11] For we who live are always given over to death because of Jesus, so that Jesus' life may also be revealed in our mortal flesh. [12] So death works in us, but life in you. [13] And since we have the same spirit of faith in keeping with what is written, I believed, therefore I spoke, we also believe, and therefore speak. [14] We know that the One who raised the Lord Jesus will raise us also with Jesus and present us with you. [15] Indeed, everything is for your benefit, so that grace, extended through more and more people, may cause thanksgiving to increase to God's glory.

[16] Therefore we do not give up. Even though our outer person is being destroyed, our inner person is being renewed day by day. [17] For our momentary light affliction is producing for us an absolutely incomparable eternal weight of glory. [18] So we do not focus on what is seen, but on what is unseen. For what is seen is temporary, but what is unseen is eternal.

WRITE A LAMENT

Use this structure, based on Psalm 71, to write your own lament. Incorporate the truth you read in today's Scripture passages, and use this time to let your heart cry out to God.

*To write a longer lament, use the notes space or use the templates in the back of this book.

INVOCATION

LORD, I SEEK _____

(what is your cry for help?)

RESCUE AND DELIVER ME, FOR YOU ARE _____

(what do you know about the character of God?)

FOR YOU _____

(what goodness has God done in the past?)

COMPLAINT

DELIVER ME FROM _____

(what is the external problem?)

FORGIVE ME FOR _____

(confess your sin; explain the internal problem)

AFFIRMATION OF TRUST

NEVERTHELESS, _____

(how can you trust in God?)

YOU ARE MY _____

(what has God promised to be?)

PETITION

SAVE ME FROM _____

(from what?)

DELIVER ME FROM _____

(what else?)

FOR YOU _____

(why should God intervene?)

STATEMENT OF CONFIDENCE

BUT I WILL _____

(how can you hope, knowing that God will hear you?)

VOW TO PRAISE

I WILL PROCLAIM _____

(what will you proclaim about God?)

I WILL SING PRAISE _____

(why will you praise God?)

10 FALLEN AND REDEEMED WORK

FALLEN WORK:

Genesis 3:17-19

Ecclesiastes 2:18-26

Romans 8:19-23

REDEEMED WORK:

Ecclesiastes 9:9-10

1 Corinthians 10:31

Colossians 3:23

Philippians 2:12-16

Work is hard. And it is also redemptive. One of the results of the fall of man was that our work was frustrated with thistles and difficulty. But God promises that He works in and through us to push back the darkness. Today's Scriptures give words to the frustration we may feel about the struggles of our work, while reminding us of how God uses His people as agents of redemption. th those who rejoice and weep with those who weep (Romans 12:15). This means we should deal honestly with both the joy and grief in life. We are called to mourn over those things worthy of lament, and we are also called to celebrate the generosity, love, and grace of God.

GENESIS 3:17-19

[17] And He said to Adam, "Because you listened to your wife's voice and ate from the tree about which I commanded you, 'Do not eat from it':

The ground is cursed because of you.
You will eat from it by means of painful labor
all the days of your life.
[18] It will produce thorns and thistles for you,
and you will eat the plants of the field.
[19] You will eat bread by the sweat of your brow
until you return to the ground,
since you were taken from it.
For you are dust,
and you will return to dust."

ECCLESIASTES 2:18-26

The Emptiness of Work

[18] I hated all my work that I labored at under the sun because I must leave it to the man who comes after me. [19] And who knows whether he will be a wise man or a fool? Yet he will take over all my work that I labored at skillfully under the sun. This too is futile. [20] So I began to give myself over to despair concerning all my work that I had labored at under the sun. [21] When there is a man whose work was done with wisdom, knowledge, and skill, and he must give his portion to a man who has not worked for it, this too is futile and a great wrong. [22] For what does a man get with all his work and all his efforts that he labors at under the sun? [23] For all his days are filled with grief, and his occupation is sorrowful; even at night, his mind does not rest. This too is futile.

[24] There is nothing better for man than to eat, drink, and enjoy his work. I have seen that even this is from God's hand, [25] because who can eat and who can enjoy life apart from Him? [26] For to the man who is pleasing in His sight, He gives wisdom, knowledge, and joy, but to the sinner He gives the task of gathering and accumulating in order to give to the one who is pleasing in God's sight. This too is futile and a pursuit of the wind.

ROMANS 8:19-23

[19] For the creation eagerly waits with anticipation for God's sons to be revealed. [20] For the creation was subjected to futility—not willingly, but because of Him who subjected it—in the hope [21] that the creation itself will also be set free from the bondage of corruption into the glorious freedom of God's children. [22] For we know that the whole creation has been groaning together with labor pains until now. [23] And not only that, but we ourselves who have the Spirit as the firstfruits—we also groan within ourselves, eagerly waiting for adoption, the redemption of our bodies.

REDEEMED WORK

ECCLESIASTES 9:9-10

[9] Enjoy life with the wife you love all the days of your fleeting life, which has been given to you under the sun, all your fleeting days. For that is your portion in life and in your struggle under the sun. [10] Whatever your hands find to do, do with all your strength...

1 CORINTHIANS 10:31

Therefore, whether you eat or drink, or whatever you do, do everything for God's glory.

Whatever you do, do it enthusiastically, as something done for the LORD and not for men...

PHILIPPIANS 2:12-16

[12] So then, my dear friends, just as you have always obeyed, not only in my presence, but now even more in my absence, work out your own salvation with fear and trembling. [13] For it is God who is working in you, enabling you both to desire and to work out His good purpose. [14] Do everything without grumbling and arguing, [15] so that you may be blameless and pure, children of God who are faultless in a crooked and perverted generation, among whom you shine like stars in the world. [16] Hold firmly to the message of life. Then I can boast in the day of Christ that I didn't run or labor for nothing.

WRITE A LAMENT

Use this structure, based on Psalm 71, to write your own lament. Incorporate the truth you read in today's Scripture passages, and use this time to let your heart cry out to God.

*To write a longer lament, use the notes space or use the templates in the back of this book.

INVOCATION

LORD, I SEEK
(what is your cry for help?)

RESCUE AND DELIVER ME, FOR YOU ARE
(what do you know about the character of God?)

FOR YOU
(what goodness has God done in the past?)

COMPLAINT

DELIVER ME FROM
(what is the external problem?)

FORGIVE ME FOR
(confess your sin; explain the internal problem)

AFFIRMATION OF TRUST

NEVERTHELESS,
(how can you trust in God?)

YOU ARE MY
(what has God promised to be?)

PETITION

SAVE ME FROM
(from what?)

DELIVER ME FROM
(what else?)

FOR YOU
(why should God intervene?)

STATEMENT OF CONFIDENCE

BUT I WILL
(how can you hope, knowing that God will hear you?)

VOW TO PRAISE

I WILL PROCLAIM
(what will you proclaim about God?)

I WILL SING PRAISE
(why will you praise God?)

NOTES

11   INJUSTICE AND JUSTICE

INJUSTICE:

Deuteronomy 16:19
Psalm 94
Hebrews 13:3

JUSTICE:

Isaiah 1:17
Psalm 68:4-10
Matthew 5:13-16
Proverbs 29:7

Justice is mentioned nearly 150 times in the Bible. The topic is important to God and, therefore, important to His people. We are called to be people whose lives are protests against injustice in the world, and one of the ways we can protest well is by mourning instances of injustice while seeking and celebrating true, biblical justice. Today's verses give us a window into God's heart concerning injustice in the world, and they also instruct us in how to pray for and desire to be conduits of justice in our own

DEUTERONOMY 16:19

"Do not deny justice or show partiality to anyone. Do not accept a bribe, for it blinds the eyes of the wise and twists the words of the righteous."

PSALM 94

The Just Judge

¹ LORD, God of vengeance—
God of vengeance, appear.
² Rise up, Judge of the earth;
repay the proud what they deserve.
³ LORD, how long will the wicked—
how long will the wicked gloat?
⁴ They pour out arrogant words;
all the evildoers boast.
⁵ LORD, they crush Your people;
they afflict Your heritage.
⁶ They kill the widow and the foreigner
and murder the fatherless.
⁷ They say, "The LORD doesn't see it.
The God of Jacob doesn't pay attention."
⁸ Pay attention, you stupid people!
Fools, when will you be wise?
⁹ Can the One who shaped the ear not hear,
the One who formed the eye not see?
¹⁰ The One who instructs nations,
the One who teaches man knowledge—
does He not discipline?

¹¹ The Lord knows man's thoughts;

they are meaningless.

¹² Lord, happy is the man You discipline

and teach from Your law

¹³ to give him relief from troubled times

until a pit is dug for the wicked.

¹⁴ The Lord will not forsake His people

or abandon His heritage,

¹⁵ for justice will again be righteous,

and all the upright in heart will follow it.

¹⁶ Who stands up for me against the wicked?

Who takes a stand for me against evildoers?

¹⁷ If the Lord had not been my helper,

I would soon rest in the silence of death.

¹⁸ If I say, "My foot is slipping,"

Your faithful love will support me, Lord.

¹⁹ When I am filled with cares,

Your comfort brings me joy.

²⁰ Can a corrupt throne—

one that creates trouble by law—

become Your ally?

²¹ They band together against the life of the righteous

and condemn the innocent to death.

²² But the Lord is my refuge;

my God is the rock of my protection.

²³ He will pay them back for their sins

and destroy them for their evil.

The Lord our God will destroy them.

HEBREWS 13:3

Remember the prisoners, as though you were in prison with them,

and the mistreated, as though you yourselves were suffering bodily.

JUSTICE

ISAIAH 1:17

"Learn to do what is good.
Seek justice.
Correct the oppressor.
Defend the rights of the fatherless.
Plead the widow's cause."

PSALM 68:4-10

4 Sing to God! Sing praises to His name.
Exalt Him who rides on the clouds—
His name is Yahweh—and rejoice before
Him.
5 God in His holy dwelling is
a father of the fatherless
and a champion of widows.
6 God provides homes for those who are
deserted.
He leads out the prisoners to prosperity,
but the rebellious live in a scorched land.

7 God, when You went out before Your
people,
when You marched through the
desert, *Selah*
8 the earth trembled and the skies poured
down rain
before God, the God of Sinai,
before God, the God of Israel.

9 You, God, showered abundant rain;
You revived Your inheritance when it
languished.
10 Your people settled in it;
God, You provided for the poor by Your
goodness.

MATTHEW 5:13-16

13 "You are the salt of the earth. But if the
salt should lose its taste, how can it be made
salty? It's no longer good for anything but
to be thrown out and trampled on by men.

14 "You are the light of the world. A city
situated on a hill cannot be hidden.
15 No one lights a lamp and puts it under
a basket, but rather on a lampstand, and
it gives light for all who are in the house.
16 In the same way, let your light shine before
men, so that they may see your good works
and give glory to your Father in heaven."

PROVERBS 29:7

The righteous person knows the rights of
the poor,
but the wicked one does not understand
these concerns.

WRITE A LAMENT

Use this structure, based on Psalm 71, to write your own lament. Incorporate the truth you read in today's Scripture passages, and use this time to let your heart cry out to God.

*To write a longer lament, use the notes space or use the templates in the back of this book.

INVOCATION

LORD, I SEEK
(what is your cry for help?)

RESCUE AND DELIVER ME, FOR YOU ARE
(what do you know about the character of God?)

FOR YOU
(what goodness has God done in the past?)

COMPLAINT

DELIVER ME FROM
(what is the external problem?)

FORGIVE ME FOR
(confess your sin; explain the internal problem)

AFFIRMATION OF TRUST

NEVERTHELESS,
(how can you trust in God?)

YOU ARE MY
(what has God promised to be?)

PETITION

SAVE ME FROM
(from what?)

DELIVER ME FROM
(what else?)

FOR YOU
(why should God intervene?)

STATEMENT OF CONFIDENCE

BUT I WILL
(how can you hope, knowing that God will hear you?)

VOW TO PRAISE

I WILL PROCLAIM
(what will you proclaim about God?)

I WILL SING PRAISE
(why will you praise God?)

NOTES

12 SOLITUDE AND COMMUNITY

SOLITUDE:
Psalm 46:10
Lamentations 3:25-28
Mark 6:30-32
Matthew 11:25-30

COMMUNITY:
Hebrews 10:23-25
Psalm 133:1
Matthew 18:20
Romans 12:4-5
Romans 12:15-19

The Christian life is personal, but it is not private. In both joy and sorrow, we sometimes need to be alone and other times need to be with people. God calls us to seasons of solitude and seasons of community. As this study draws to a close, may we have the courage to seek both. May this journey through Scripture grant us the freedom to mourn our losses and celebrate our joys both privately and publicly. We are never alone. God is faithful, and He is with us. Lean on Christ and His church. He promises to give us rest and be our joy.

PSALM 46:10 ESV

"Be still, and know that I am God.
  I will be exalted among the nations,
  I will be exalted in the earth!"

LAMENTATIONS 3:25-28

25 The LORD is good to those who wait for Him,
to the person who seeks Him.
26 It is good to wait quietly
for deliverance from the LORD.
27 It is good for a man to bear the yoke
while he is still young.

28 Let him sit alone and be silent,
for God has disciplined him.

MARK 6:30-32

30 The apostles gathered around Jesus and reported to Him all that they had done and taught. 31 He said to them, "Come away by yourselves to a remote place and rest for a while." For many people were coming and going, and they did not even have time to eat. 32 So they went away in the boat by themselves to a remote place...

MATTHEW 11:25-30

The Son Gives Knowledge and Rest

25 At that time Jesus said, "I praise You, Father, Lord of heaven and earth, because You have hidden these things from the wise and

learned and revealed them to infants. [26] Yes, Father, because this was Your good pleasure. [27] All things have been entrusted to Me by My Father. No one knows the Son except the Father, and no one knows the Father except the Son and anyone to whom the Son desires to reveal Him.

[28] "Come to Me, all of you who are weary and burdened, and I will give you rest. [29] All of you, take up My yoke and learn from Me, because I am gentle and humble in heart, and you will find rest for yourselves. [30] For My yoke is easy and My burden is light."

COMMUNITY

HEBREWS 10:23-25 ESV

[23] Let us hold fast the confession of our hope without wavering, for he who promised is faithful. [24] And let us consider how to stir up one another to love and good works, [25] not neglecting to meet together, as is the habit of some, but encouraging one another, and all the more as you see the Day drawing near.

PSALM 133:1

How good and pleasant it is
when brothers live together in harmony!

MATTHEW 18:20

"For where two or three are gathered together in My name, I am there among them."

[4] Now as we have many parts in one body, and all the parts do not have the same function, [5] in the same way we who are many are one body in Christ and individually members of one another.

...

[15] Rejoice with those who rejoice; weep with those who weep. [16] Be in agreement with one another. Do not be proud; instead, associate with the humble. Do not be wise in your own estimation. [17] Do not repay anyone evil for evil. Try to do what is honorable in everyone's eyes. [18] If possible, on your part, live at peace with everyone. [19] Friends, do not avenge yourselves; instead, leave room for Hiswrath. For it is written: Vengeance belongs to Me; I will repay, says the Lord.

WRITE A LAMENT

Use this structure, based on Psalm 71, to write your own lament. Incorporate the truth you read in today's Scripture passages, and use this time to let your heart cry out to God.

*To write a longer lament, use the notes space or use the templates in the back of this book.

INVOCATION

LORD, I SEEK _____

(what is your cry for help?)

RESCUE AND DELIVER ME, FOR YOU ARE _____

(what do you know about the character of God?)

FOR YOU _____

(what goodness has God done in the past?)

COMPLAINT

DELIVER ME FROM _____

(what is the external problem?)

FORGIVE ME FOR _____

(confess your sin; explain the internal problem)

AFFIRMATION OF TRUST

NEVERTHELESS, _____

(how can you trust in God?)

YOU ARE MY _____

(what has God promised to be?)

PETITION

SAVE ME FROM _____

(from what?)

DELIVER ME FROM _____

(what else?)

FOR YOU _____

(why should God intervene?)

STATEMENT OF CONFIDENCE

BUT I WILL _____

(how can you hope, knowing that God will hear you?)

VOW TO PRAISE

I WILL PROCLAIM _____

(what will you proclaim about God?)

I WILL SING PRAISE _____

(why will you praise God?)

13 GRACE DAY

Use this day to pray, rest, and reflect on this week's reading, giving thanks for the grace that is ours in Christ.

Focusing on the second part of verse 4, ask the Holy Spirit for the freedom to mourn and dance in every season of your life.

There is an occasion for everything,
and a time for every activity under
heaven:

a time to weep and a time to laugh;
a time to mourn and a time to dance.

ECCLESIASTES 3:1,4

NOTES

14 WEEKLY TRUTH

Scripture is God-breathed and true. When we memorize it, we carry the gospel with us wherever we go.

"Therefore, whether you eat or drink,
or whatever you do,
do everything for God's glory."

INVOCATION

COMPLAINT

AFFIRMATION
OF TRUST

PETITION

STATEMENT OF
CONFIDENCE

VOW
TO PRAISE

INVOCATION

COMPLAINT

AFFIRMATION
OF TRUST

PETITION

STATEMENT OF
CONFIDENCE

VOW
TO PRAISE

VOW
TO PRAISE

STATEMENT OF
CONFIDENCE

PETITION

AFFIRMATION
OF TRUST

COMPLAINT

INVOCATION

INVOCATION

COMPLAINT

AFFIRMATION
OF TRUST

PETITION

STATEMENT OF
CONFIDENCE

VOW
TO PRAISE

VOW
TO PRAISE

STATEMENT OF
CONFIDENCE

PETITION

AFFIRMATION
OF TRUST

COMPLAINT

INVOCATION

Where did I study?

□ HOME   □ SCHOOL
□ OFFICE   □ COFFEE SHOP
□ CHURCH   □ OTHER:

_____

_____

WHAT WAS I LISTENING TO?

Song: _____

Artist: _____

Album: _____

_____

What time of day did I study?

□ MORNING
□ AFTERNOON
□ NIGHT
□ OTHER:

_____

_____

What was happening in the world?

_____

_____

_____

_____

What was happening in my life?

_____

_____

_____

_____

_____

_____

MY CLOSING PRAYER:

_____

END DATE

_____ / _____ / _____